Write Like The Wolf

8-Figure Copywriting Secrets

*"The real life processes, routines, tips & hacks
that helped me generate over 8-Figures
for my clients in just 12 months."*

Cover Design by: Ryan Ross

Published by The Writer's Fix in
Marina del Rey, CA
www.TheWritersFix.com

For More Information, Please Contact:
Cole@writelikethewolf.com

Published in the United States of America

VanDeWoestyne, Cole (Author)
Write Like The Wolf
ISBN-13: 9781728842448

First edition published in
the United States, January 2019

Distributed by KDP, an Amazon company.

"Everything in life is worth writing about. You just have to believe in yourself enough to find your story and share it with the world."

Cole VanDeWoestyne

Disclaimer

Copy is extremely powerful. If you're making extreme claims or if you're writing in highly regulated industries such as business opportunity or the financial space be sure to get a full legal review from an FTC experienced attorney after you write, but before you use your copy. You and solely you are responsible for how you use what you learn inside this very book.

Now that is out of the way...
You may flip the page if you understand
and agree with the disclaimer.

Table of Contents

Section One: The Induction

Section Two: The Foundation

Section Three: The Million $$$ Set-up

Section Four: How To . . .

Section Five: Outbox $$$

From The Author

I want to *genuinely* congratulate you on **investing in yourself**, your clients, your family, your well . . .

. . . everything.

If you're a *World Class Copywriter* already and you're using this book as reference material *don't worry*. You'll pick up one or two or even three new tricks to add to your tool belt. You know as well as anyone that the more tools at your disposal, the more *powerful your impact.*

For those of you that are brand new to copywriting which I'm sure most of you are, don't be fooled by that above statement.

This book was written specifically for you to leverage the skills taught inside to absolutely explode your knowledge and impact in your own business and for your clients businesses.

When you made the decision to purchase this book that is in your hands right now, you made the decision to improve your life forever.

Now, this isn't going to be a book about all that rah-rah motivational shit that gets you all pumped up and left with absolutely no knowledge for you to use to succeed.

This book was written specifically to help you improve your creativity, writing, persuasion, communication, and most importantly conversions.

I want to share with you exactly who this book was written for and how you can leverage it to its full potential.

It will take a few minutes to read but will be one of the most *powerful* parts of this book as it will set you up for your future success.

Re: The spark of an idea

From the hypothetical desk of Cole VanDeee

Dear future copy genius,

When I mention my "hypothetical desk" above I mean it. As copywriters, marketers, and entrepreneurs our dream is to run as far away from a desk as possible. We want to travel the world and live life to the fullest.

This book will help you do exactly that if you're willing to invest the time, energy, and effort required to make it to that level. The <u>good news</u> is that if you've made it this far already I feel pretty confident that you're going to do just fine.

But I do have to be honest with you . . .

This book was written not for you, but for me. I wrote this book for myself. Not because I'm selfish, a little selfish maybe, but because I wish I knew everything I'm about to share with you when I first got started. I'm secretly hoping that I can travel back in time like Marty in his Delorean and give this book to myself right before I began copywriting professionally.

I would have saved a lot of time, energy, effort, money, embarrassment, frustration, and more importantly my sanity.

So that's what this book is for. It's to help you save time, money, and frustration. You're going to learn everything you need to know when it comes to writing copy that captures your reader's eye and converts them into a lifelong fan.

When you're finished reading this book you're going to have such a solid foundation of copywriting and persuasion with the written word that you're actually going to want to quit your job and launch a copywriting agency.

If you're already running advertising you're going to erase all of your funnel copy. You're going to rewrite all of your video scripts. All of your follow up emails? You'll toss them. It's *basically* a guarantee.

As if that wasn't enough . . .

You're going to **increase** your *conversions* while you lower *your* ad spend. Well, at least you *should*. I know my clients and I have both shared these same results hundreds and hundreds of times over again. Although my results may not be "typical" or "normal" I am living proof that they **are possible**.

I, however, can **<u>NOT</u>** control the effort, time, and energy placed into the mastering the art and techniques that are going to be laid out in this book.

What I can tell you is this:

If you don't put in the work, study, reread and absolutely obsess over this book . . . You **WILL NOT** see results <u>**AND**</u> this will be a *complete waste of your time.*

So, take notes. Re-read some chapters. Study this as if you're sitting in a classroom at Harvard. I can only imagine the beautiful words that you'll begin to create and share with your audience so they can relate with you better so they're comfortable enough to invest in you, your programs, and any other products or services you may offer.

If you're willing to invest your time, energy, and effort today . . .

. . . you'll reap the rewards tomorrow.

SECTION ONE
THE INDUCTION

CHAPTER ONE
THE WOLF OF COPYWRITING

When you think of a wolf what picture comes to mind? Maybe that particular wolf is roaming around in a snowy forest or hanging around in a pack of wolves about to prey on their next meal.

However,

When I picture a wolf I **don't** picture an aggressive animal that's trying to eat anything and everything it can. I see the wolf *much differently*.

If you've ever studied the behavior patterns of wolves you know that wolves are often considered the most loyal and protective species that we're blessed enough to share this earth with.

After really diving into how wolves truly act I couldn't get away from integrating wolves into *my future*.

Although that future could lead me down thousands even tens of thousands of different paths, I know at the end of the day that my vision is to create a tight nit wolf pack that is loyal and protective of each other forcing one another to grow each and every single day.

So, how can all of us with such different backgrounds join forces inside of this new Wolf Pack?

We all face a lot of the same challenges. In fact, I recently discovered this over the last few years.

After a lot of brainstorming, masterminds, seminars, meetings, and who knows how much money (I stopped counting at $100,000) I believe I have discovered the secret to impacting the world at scale. (and it's not what you think...)

If you're here reading this book right now it's because you're either a copywriter, marketer, or entrepreneur. (or you want to be)

It's a pretty **BIG DEAL.**

Let me explain . . .

Copywriters are the voice behind the brands that shape our world. Without copywriters we wouldn't have the massive economy we have today.

Marketers place that same voice in front of millions of people to help solve problems in their lives. <u>Without</u> marketers, no one would hear about the solutions entrepreneurs have created.

Entrepreneurs had the vision of the business in the first place and the ability to put all the pieces together to continue evolving the world in a positive way.

The three of us together shape and shift the world and bend the rules to make it work in our favor.

As we begin to form this new wolf pack together, we need to stick together. Remain loyal and help each other reach the levels of success we've always dreamt of.

None of us can build the empires we dream of on our own. This wolf pack will help support you with the foundation we all need to create our own individual empires.

If we remain loyal and protective over our pack, we will become unstoppable on our mission of impacting the world.

Consider this book my personal invitation to you in hopes that you'll have no choice but to say YES and join the Wolf Pack.

CHAPTER TWO
WHAT TO EXPECT

How many books have you personally picked up and read throughout your lifetime?

Take a moment to think.

Now,

Take a moment to think about how many books you read cover to cover.

I remember reading a statistic somewhere, but can't seem to find it again (or I'm too lazy to look it up.) However, that statistic I remember as being something crazy like 95% of people that pick up a book never finish it. Is it true? Maybe. Is this a common problem the world faces?

Absolutely.

Especially when it comes to the self-help category. There can be a number of reasons why this statistic proves to be true. From personal experience and I'm sure you'll agree with me on this one, but most self-help books don't lay out a clear path of precisely what will be happening throughout the entire book.

Most people lose interest right before the good stuff starts to come out and that's why millions and millions of books are published each year, but yet you could walk over to just about anyone's bookshelf and see piles and piles of dust on their books they never finished.

In my attempt to bring you as much value as possible I've manufactured a strategy to give you good information on every single page of this book that will keep you not only engaged but excited to implement what you learn in your own business.

Think of this book as your study guide, dictionary, reference material, and Ivy

League education. I want you to get the absolute most out of this book.

As I sit here and write this right now I can remember my English teacher from my sophomore year in High School. She always told us to highlight and take notes within the books we pick up.

She mentioned that it helps our brain not only retain the information or story that we are reading, but it's much easier to go back and skim to find the important information.

I encourage you to do the same.

When you see something that sucks you in and pushes your mind into a new state of being,

STOP.

Live in that moment. It's those moments that help sculpt our future to look more and more like our dreams.

Before I send you off into the **massive world** of copywriting I want to *paint* a picture of what reading this book will look like for you . . .

I do this not because you can't picture it yourself, but because understanding the full vision before experiencing the journey will allow you to fully immerse yourself into your readings and retain much more knowledge on a much *deeper level*. Afterall, that's what we're here for right?

Section one will be inducting you into the world of copywriting. You learned a little bit about me in the previous chapter. In this chapter you'll be uncovering what to expect through this book so you can truly maximize every page to its fullest potential.

Section two you'll learn why A-List copywriter's do what they do in the way they do it. You'll have the opportunity to really see the *behind the scenes* of a real-life copywriter and fully understand what crosses their mind on a daily basis.

Shifting into the "Copywriter's Mindset" will allow you to fully **eliminate** writer's block.

For those of you who don't have these challenges, **please don't skip this chapter.** Just having a new perspective on how the best copywriter's in the world think will give you the edge that you're searching for.

When you transition into the next few chapters you'll begin understanding what a proper writing process looks like. I've included some extra steps I take outside of actually sitting down to write.

Some of these "extra steps" will allow you to *break free* and really force yourself to **pour** creativity from your fingers *without* any effort. They include things like meditation, creativity hacks, and some other tips and tricks no one else has taught you.

These extra tips are enough to turn anyone into a B-List copywriter. However, it's the writing process that will take you into **A-List status.**

I'll be breaking down my own process so you know **exactly** what to put where and why.

Having a process is how you *duplicate results*. No more shooting in the dark. You'll be able to look down the sights of your new weapon and strike a bullseye every single time.

As you can imagine, that process won't do you any good if you don't have a strategy to back it up. A bulletproof process can only take you so far.

In Section Three you'll discover how to select the right approach to writing your copy. Do you need to be aggressive? Softer with more emotion?

Longer and more informative? Or short and to the point?

Knowing how to select the proper approach will increase anyone's conversions. As copywriters sometimes we need to steer the ship to help our clients to the best of our ability.

Generally, you'll find the proper approach after you've researched your audience. You'll be learning where to find them and how to find their specific trigger words.

Every audience set has their own specific trigger words that can get them to do anything. Uncovering these could mean the difference between a million dollar campaign and a million dollar bust.

By this point you'll have the process, the strategy, and know exactly how to conduct your research.

Now for the important part.

Section Four: How to…

There are numerous ways you can now execute writing ad copy. During this section of the book

you will learn the slight tweaks and adjustments to the strategies, research, and process you need in order to execute properly.

A webinar script will be much different than a VSL. This section will be breaking down the differences and how to properly execute when writing each individual piece.

In Section Five we talk about Outbox $$$. Mark Cuban said it best, it's "F U" money. The Fuck You money is created in the Follow Up (F U.) Most believe Fuck You money mean having so much money that you can literally look anyone in the face and say "Fuck You" and have the funds to back it up.

So this section is going to scrape the remains of who you don't sell through your original copy and put them back into the funnel so they will buy.

There are also some bonuses at the very end, but I'm not going to talk much about those here because you really need to follow this page by page, word by word and consume everything you see and read.

This book could be considered the McLaren of books.

Here's why:

There are faster, stronger and "cooler" cars. But when you look under the hood it's a mess. Disorganized and really only designed to be fun while you use it and to show off to others. But the real crisp clean intentional design that allows you to completely fall in love with every single piece of the puzzle from the original idea, to the hand crafted parts to firing up the engine in your garage every single day...

...that's what gets you going.

CHAPTER 3
MAXIMIZING THIS BOOK

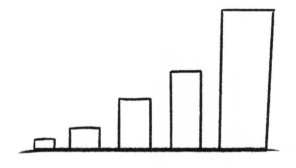

I really want to be candid with you in this first paragraph. The **majority** of people who read through this book will do *nothing* with the information. The data supports that. However, I firmly believe **you** sitting there right **now** know and understand that this book can and will change your life if you use it.

> *"Your Why Has To Be*
> *Greater Than Your Pain."*
> Dr. Eric Thomas

The reason you're reading this book is going to be much different than someone sitting halfway across the world, but from a top down view it's the same.

You picked up a copy of Write Like The Wolf because something needed to change.

I'll take another page out of Eric Thomas' motivational career.

Think of someone you love and care about. It could be your husband, wife, kids, mother, brother, sister, aunt, uncle . . . anyone. Think of them right now.

Are you doing this so you can provide a better life for them?

I know you are.

I know this because I'm writing this because of the people I love are depending on me.

I wake up and think about them every single morning. My goal isn't to push this book into millions of peoples hands, but to change the statistics that are working against the majority.

I know that my WHY is so powerful and contagious that just the pure energy of you coming across my book from a friend, family member, co-worked, advertisement, bookstore... etc it was simply meant to be.

I mentioned earlier that most people won't use the information they learn in this book.

We need this book to stand out and be different.

You need to use it.

So everytime you wake up, think of those people you love.

Remember that the knowledge from this book is going to provide those people with a *better quality of life*.

I have spent nearly a year just planning out how to lay out the content inside of this book.

I've received insight from NY Times Best Sellers. I've received insight from those who coach Billionaires. I've received insight from neuro scientists. I've received insight from data analysts. I've structured this book in such a way that YOU WILL be able to consume this content and implement it into your daily life.

Here's the thing, you **CANNOT** read this book in one or two days.

You **CANNOT** read this book in a week.

You **CANNOT** read this book in 1 month.

You must invest the time to read this book and implement it properly.

So how on earth do you do that?

*That's what I'm going to share
with you right now . . .*

- Read this 1 chapter at a time
- Spend 20-30 minutes a day reading
- 10-15 minutes writing down how you can implement it
- Re-read the chapter and revise/add to what you had previously wrote down

Doing these steps precisely will help ensure you're able to properly implement each and every piece of information within this book.

Remember, this needs to be the book that resets the statistics other books have allowed to happen.

Can we count on you?

SECTION TWO
THE FOUNDATION

CHAPTER 4
THE COPYWRITER'S MINDSET

Copywriting is so much more than simply placing words on a page. It requires a full understanding of how humans think.

This is one of those chapters that you'll want to read over and over again until you have every word memorized.

After nearly a decade of obsessing over how the human mind works I'm finally sitting down, summarizing, and laying out the most important tips, tricks, hacks, and every other powerful piece of information I've learned over the years.

My hope is that you take the information within this chapter and begin the process of applying it to every aspect of your life. Remember, you're not just learning how to write better copy, you're learning how to think like a copywriter. Constantly analyzing human behavior in real life and online.

"In real life, what do you mean?"

Thinking like a copywriter isn't a switch you can turn on and off. Once your mindset is transformed into a powerful copywriting machine you won't be able to switch it off.

I remember not too long ago I was asked to speak at a Mastermind in Seattle to speak on copywriting. After the event we broke out into mini sessions where people were able to sit with whichever speaker they wanted to and ask more in-depth questions.

As we were sitting in our little group of 4 or 5 people the same question kept popping up over and over again. "What do you study to write such powerful ad copy?" I replied with "people." Then I started giving them examples.

I pointed at a few of the attendees who weren't retaining any information that was being given to them. Their body language and glazed over eyes told me this. I pointed at one of the speakers who is overly passionate about helping others. I simply said "Look at how passionate he is and all of his energy, he keeps using the phrase "my clients" he really loves to show off his client results rather than boast about his own. His copy most likely reflects more testimonials than anything else.

You don't need to be at a mastermind to pick up how humans are reacting. The next time you're at a restaurant eating, look around and find two or more people having conversations. Try and guess what the conversation is about without listening, but just watching. Their facial expressions and body language will tell you everything you need to know.

"But how does reading body language help you write better copy?"

Some of the best marketers in the world will tell you that testing is crucial for success. Reading reactions, facial expressions and body language is your real life testing. You can use a series of trigger words in a conversation or maybe use one of your headlines for a VSL page as a question to someone you've just met.

My belief here is that copywriters aren't necessarily copywriters, but instead psychology experts who bend the human mind to wrap around their idea or concept they need to sell in an ethical manner.

The good news is that you don't need some fancy psychology degree for you to develop this mindset. Honestly, I only made it three weeks in college before I ran far, far, far away to never return. So don't believe for one second that you need to be a college graduate to figure this stuff out.

I have a few very precise steps you'll need to retrain your mind so you can access your inner copywriter and unleash that powerful persuasiveness that's been hiding inside you.

Step 1: The Morning Routine

I didn't reinvent the wheel at all here. I actually stole my morning routine from one of my past clients Alex Charfen and The Billionaire Code.[1]

Although mine is just slightly different than Alex's, most of it remains the same. And yours may be slightly different as well, but having a morning routine is the most important piece here.

Here it is:

1.   Wake up at the SAME time EVERYDAY
2.   Get up & Moving Instantly
3.   Hyper-Hydrate (32 oz of water)
4.   Meditate
5.   Primal Walk
6.   Write

It may seem simple or easy or strange to you, but every step in that routine has its individual purpose.

Waking up at the same time everyday regardless of what time you go to sleep forces your body into a routine. Reducing the trauma your body experiences going from a dead sleep to awake and using it's brain is the key element here.

Get up and moving. This gets the blood flowing and lets your body know that you're okay and ready to tackle the day.

Hyperhydration is so important. This removes the flight or fright your body experiences when it wakes up. It lets your body know that you're here, you're okay, and that you're thriving.

Meditating clears any possibility of negative thoughts and allows for a clear mind to begin your day.

Your primal walk will ground you with the earth. This is a barefoot walk outside for 15-20 minutes. No phone, no music, no anything. Just you, the ground, the world. Enjoy your surroundings and really feel your own energy becoming one with the world around you.

Whatever variation of this morning routine you adopt will work. The idea is to create the routine so your brain can dump all of the clutter at night while you're sleeping and wake up properly without stress.

Knowing exactly what you're going to do for the first 20-30 minutes of the day without thinking about it truly helps get your mind and body going.

After you have completely cleared your mind and finished your routine it's time to write. There's a very easy way to make this happen for you without having writer's block and I want to share it with you right now.

Here's what it could look like for you:

It's morning time still and you just came back from your walk. You hyper-hydrate once more to replace the fluids that had left your body. You grab a glass of water and sit down with your laptop.

As you open your laptop you begin to think of topics or ideas. Maybe today you can't put your finger on what you want to write about.

So you open up a tab on your browser and find yourself on a stock image website. You know, one of those free ones. As you shift through the images you finally have an idea about you want to write about and without thinking much more you open up a fresh google doc to begin typing.

You don't worry about grammar or spelling. And honestly, you don't care if what you're writing even makes sense.

You're simply allowing your brain to dump all of its thoughts onto the page word by word. Maybe today you dumped out a few hundred words or even a few thousand.

The idea is that you're not writing a project or funnel copy or anything for that matter. You're simply allowing your mind to roam free.

Once you can allow your mind to run free every single day you'll begin to notice how much more clear your thoughts and ideas are.

This . . .

This is the foundation of a copywriters mind.

However, this doesn't even begin to scratch the surface of the copywriters mindset.

What I'm about to share with you could possibly be one of the most significant pieces of information you'll read in this book.

Perspective

Write that word down or highlight it if you haven't already. Perspective can be the *difference* from a campaign that flops from one that *pulls down millions like clock work.*

When we write copy for funnels, blogs, websites, advertising… etc we <u>aren't</u> writing the copy for ourselves.

Remember that saying from when you were younger?

> " *Put yourself in their shoes and imagine what they're feeling.*"

We have to use this same concept everytime we sit down at a computer, laptop or have a notepad in our hand. *Anytime* we begin to put words together for others to read we **must** think "what will the reader think, feel and want after reading this?"

I have an exercise that I teach inside of **Write Like The Wolf Academy** that helps my students immediately eliminate the bad habit of writing from their own perspective.

Exercise: I to You

Objective:

To clearly and easily understand how to flip the perspective of a story from *your* perspective into **your readers perspective.**

Benefits:

Increased reader engagement. Extract deep human emotional connection with ease.

Takeaways:

The ability to recognize the perspective you're *currently writing in* and **flipping** it in a way that is more beneficial for not only you, but for your reader as well.

This isn't going to be structured in a way that you would learn inside a classroom at Harvard . . .

In fact,

This may be a little unorthodox, but please stick with me as it is proven to work tremendously well and has brought results to many people across the globe.

First:

Visit writelikethewolf.com/IvsYou

There you will find a link to download two PDFs. You will need both! (yes they're FREE.)

Second:

Read through the PDF that is titled: "I"

Take notes on where the story was powerful and make suggestions on how you would make it better.

Third:

Read through the PDF that is titled: "You"

Take notes on where the store was powerful and make suggestions on how you would make it better.

Fourth:

Now compare the two. Which one do you believe was the more powerful story? Which one made you more emotional? Which one really extracted every ounce of creativity and vulnerability from you?

Challenges:

Often times I hear students (and even find myself time to time) trying to force a perspective out knowing full well I could drum up thousands of words if I simply wrote from my own perspective.

This can create frustration and even worse . . .

Writer's Block.

Solution:

Write in the perspective that is easiest for the words to flow. You can easily revisit the copy and flip the story. It adds an additional layer of work, but can oftentimes lead to your best work. So don't get discouraged because you have to edit your own work. Get excited.

*Your next brilliant idea is one edit away from being the piece of copy **EVERY** marketer is talking about.*

CHAPTER 5
WHY WE USE A PROCESS

Can you imagine going through life without a process? Think about this for a second.

Do you wake up around the same time everyday?

Do you eat around the same times every day?

Do you brush your teeth around the same time every day?

Our lives have become a process not through instinct . . .

But because of how we were raised.

A process does not fall out of the sky and become naturally stuck in your brain. You must create the process, believe in the process and implement the process.

Those that came before us who had laid the path to success also left a process. As each entrepreneur got ahold of this path they began to make tweaks, changes and additions to fit their molding.

It's been hundreds of years since that first process was discovered and it's been passed down generation by generation. Improved upon, tidied up and flat out simplified.

So how can we leverage this observation and use it to our advantage?

Well, by building our own process as a copywriter of course.

Copywriting has been around for some time now. In fact, I personally can trace it back to the year of 1493.

No, that is not a type-o by any means. That is the correct year. Over 500 years ago the first direct response copywriter released his first piece.

Do you know the person I am referring to?

If not don't worry. It took me quite a bit of time to dig up this person.

Aldus Manutius.

He founded Aldine Press. Thought to be the very first person in history to make books available to the public.

After weeks of research and translating I have finally uncovered the positioning from the very first sales letter ever written.

So what on earth does this have to do with a copywriter's process?

EVERYTHING.

Aldus had a very specific process he followed to achieve the end goal he had envisioned of putting books into the hands of everyone in the world.

The process that Aldus used is the same process marketers are using today to generate ridiculous amount of revenue, but more importantly change the world at scale.

So what was Aldus' marketing process?

Step 1: Discovering The Needs

Aldus had uncovered a problem that many of his neighbors and friends shared. They didn't have access to books and if they did they were too large to carry with them.

Step 2: Testing The Market

Aldus set out throughout his town and began asking everyone who would listen if they would indeed like this problem he had uncovered to be solved. He discovered who his target audience was going to be. How old they were, what economic class they were in and what their interests were.

Step 3: Form The Idea

Aldus didn't just produce any books, but he produced the most important books to those who were extremely interested in carrying a smaller, lighter and more durable book with them. His idea began to form.

Step 4: Position The Offer

Once Aldus had uncovered the problem, asked others if they wanted this problem solved and then solidified his offer he knew exactly how to position his offer. He would drum up an offer and mail everyone in town a letter letting them know the books were available.

Step 5: Scale It

Just a few short years after Aldus released his first re-printed book into the world orders began to fly off the shelves. People began wanting more and more books by more and more authors. Word quickly spread and his company took off.

Conclusion:

So if this is a marketing process that is still being used today what does it have to do with our copywriting process?

Well . . .

Everything and nothing at the same exact time.

But understanding how companies put products out into the world will help tremendously when writing your copy.

So let's break down the copywriter's process now...

Fair enough? (one of my favorite questions to place in my copy)

The process itself is fairly simple.

The 8-Figure Copywriting Process:

If you follow this process you will succeed with your copy 100% of the time. If you *skipped* to this chapter and missed the chapter on mindset, **please go back.** This will **not** work without the proper mindset.

Step 1: End Goal

"Begin with the end in mind" -- Stephen Covey

When you fully understand what outcome you need to happen you hold all of the power you need in order to execute your plan. You hear

entrepreneurs like Gary Vee say things like . . .
"Reverse Engineer stuff." The idea is that if you
understand what you want to happen you will be
able to lay down the path to make it come to
fruition.

Step 2: Audience

You've determined your end goal. Who is going to
see that end goal through? What person is going to
follow you from point A to point B and scream
"Yes, I have to have that!"

Your audience is important because this is where
you'll do your research for the next step.

Step 3: Fact Finding

This is where the gold is. The late Gary Halbert
was even believed to go door to door sampling his
copy verbally to random victims who would listen
to his pitch. He would analyze their face and
determine where the emotions began to come out.

With the digital world you don't have to go door to
door. But picking up the phone isn't a bad idea or

even testing a small audience with your idea. Ask questions, poke around, read books, find articles and newspaper clippings, check on what's trending and most importantly ENGAGE!

You'll begin to uncover the pain points that your audience has and what drives them to buy. What emotions are needed?

Step 4: Craft Your Offer

Once you've completed your research you should have a very good idea of who your target audience is, what drives them to by, what their pain point is and how they want to be sold.

With this information you'll put your offer together. Your offer should be understood by someone who has NEVER heard of your industry, product, service, business, or anything.

A child should be able to read your offer and understand exactly what they're going to get and why they need it right now.

Step 5: Craft Your Story

Every story has a beginning, middle and end. Right?

You'll need to include the following:

➢ Hook (Get them interested)
➢ Relate (Keep them interested)
➢ Transition (Tell Your Story)
➢ Wrecking Ball (Tear Down Objections)
➢ "AHA" Moment (The Selling Point)
➢ Offer (The Offer You Created)
➢ *PS . . . (Last Chance To Grab A Sale)*

Step 6: Edit Edit Edit

Once you have it all put together walk away from it for a few days. Don't think about it anymore.

Alright, it's day three and you're ready to look at your beautiful masterpiece. The good news is that it's not permanent.

Now it's time to tear your copy apart.

Gently.

You don't want to over think anything. You'll just want to quickly skim through and find words you could swap out for things that are easier to read. (A shortcut for this is the hemingway app. It tells you the grade level you wrote at.)

You want your copy to be read between a 4th and 6th grade level.

Think about it, if it's too challenging to read people will get frustrated and move on.

It's rare that someone goes "This is way too complicated to read, I should purchase whatever they're selling and figure it out."

So keep it simple.

And that's the process laid out!

Your biggest take away:

Follow The Process.

CHAPTER 6
WHY COPYWRITERS EXIST

Before we can really dive in and start the real writing process we have to break down why copywriters even exist in the first place.

The obvious answer is *"we need people who write advertising."*

The deeper answer is not quite as simple.

This chapter will lay out why copywriters exist and why we are so damn important.

If it sounds egotistical, that's because it is.

You'll have a pretty good understanding of why that is and why we are so damn unapologetic about it too.

So flip this page, embark on a journey that very few will take on... but for those that do will forever remember this moment.

I've said it before and I'll continue to say it.

Copy is powerful.

It always has been and always will be.

Here's why...

A good copywriter isn't necessarily a good "writer" by any means. In fact, most of us were awful in school. English was most likely a challenge and the thought of becoming a professional writer was never really a thought.

Our grammar is usually pretty poor and our spelling probably isn't great and our vocabulary is pretty weak to say the least.

So how on earth do we become copywriters?

For some of us we were sales people. Others were entrepreneurs. Some of us come from random jobs and others fall into it accidentally.

The common theme amongst us? We have accidentally uncovered the power of copy.

We recognized the significant impact it can leave on the world and the real reason behind it all...

> *...the money we print with every single word we write.*

It's extremely rare that you're able to sit at a laptop anywhere in the world (you don't even need internet) and put words to paper and pull out millions of dollars for your clients and yourself.

This is a key ingredient to why this skill has stayed around for as long as it has.

Let's look at the world and what's really important in reality.

Please keep in mind that this is reality, not what should or shouldn't be "right" or "wrong." So if you get offended easily, you've been warned.

The one thing that keeps the world spinning is money. Money drives all four pillars of life. Health, Love, Wisdom and Wealth.

Now don't get me wrong, you can lead a very healthy, loved filled life with lots and lots of wisdom for absolutely no money. But you must accept that lifestyle and live off the grid and be 100% self sufficient or find a village that shares the same values as you.

For the rest of us we strive to lead a very healthy, love filled life with an abundance of wisdom and money. Eating healthy is more expensive than eating unhealthy. Dating can be tough when the stress of not having enough money is weighing on the both of you. And learning is expensive with the wrong perspective.

Money is the driving force behind the world and how it operates.

Without copywriters... businesses wouldn't be able to stand out, share their story and sell their customers.

Businesses need to stand out because businesses are the constant drive of change and innovation in our world. If you look throughout history you'll see that entrepreneurs just like you have been paving the way for us to continue building, growing and evolving into the incredible creatures that we all are today.

If businesses can't stand out, share their story and sell their customers...

> *...we simply would stop evolving and eventually would all become extinct.*

Think of Martin Luther King Jr. for a moment when you think of someone who used the power of persuasion and copy to continue and push forward the Civil Rights movement of the 1900's that has evolved into our society in coming together no matter the race, religion or beliefs of another human being.

We still have a long way to go, but when you look back... you realize how far we've come

If it wasn't for the powerful words strategically placed in Dr. King's speeches would he have left as big of an impact as he did?

Would we be living in the same world we are today? Or would we simply be living in the world that Dr. King grew up in?

Sounds humble doesn't it? Implying that copy is the sole reason the world changes...

...and honestly it couldn't be further from the truth.

We'll talk about that later on in the book. For now?

Just understand that copy will drive both the good and bad ideas, opportunities, offers, products, services, businesses, political campaigns... and anything else you could think of forward to continue the evolution that has been set forth by the originator.

So be wise with how you use these skills. This book will drill into your conscious and subconscious, because you very well could change the world after reading this book that is currently sitting in your hands.

It is up to you to decide how you will use this powerful skill and apply it into the world that you live in.

I trust you will make the right decision.

Section Three:
The Million $ Set Up

CHAPTER 7
THE ONE THING

I needed to start this section with a brief, but important tactic that if executed properly will make the rest of this book easier to apply and have your copy converting like crazy.

As you saw above, the title is "The One Thing."

Now, A lot of you understand what this means. Which is AWFUL. Please throw away any and everything you think you may or may not know about "The One Thing" and allow me to introduce my own perspective.

Fair enough?

In marketing a lot of times you're told that you need to focus on just one product or service. And this is completely and 100% true.

However, for copy it's completely different.

Here's what I mean:

When we write our copy we must focus on the next step.

Example:

Let's say you're selling a digital course on how to throw a baseball like a seasoned MLB pro.

You now have a funnel that gets them all the way to the course. Your funnel probably looks a lot like this: .

You have to look at each piece of this as selling one thing.

Your Facebook Ad is not selling the digital course. Your Facebook ad is selling the click.

Your landing page for the Free eBook is selling the Free eBook.

Your landing page for the Mini Course is selling the Mini Course.

Your landing page for the Digital Course is selling the Digital Course.

Where most people fail is that they try to sell them on needing the digital course before they opt in and grab the Free eBook.

So in this chapter when we talk about The One Thing what we're talking about is how to stay focused on the goal at hand for the specific copy we are writing. What's that pieces job and how can I position each piece to sell the next step?

Let's break this down to the nitty gritty so you have a full understanding of what this all actually looks like.

Before you begin you must think about the ultimate outcome for your perfect prospect. What does it look like for them? Are they moved all the way into your or your clients elite inner circle? Or do you or they not have one? What's the true end goal here?

Now you can begin reverse engineering and thinking, "okay, I know where I want them to go what is the best way to get them there?"

So walk yourself backwards and map out every step of the way.

Now as a copywriter or someone writing their own copy you can focus on each of those steps. Think of it as if you were building a spiral staircase for your home. You can't get to the next step unless you believe it's there right?

Think about that more deeply for a second. Think to a time where you were in someone else's home for the very first time and you have to walk up or down stairs in the dark where you couldn't see anything. Pretty scary right? Legs might have shaken a little bit. You most likely would feel around with your hands or feet trying to find the edges and making sure there was a step there.

It's that confidence that the next step is going to support you and be there when you need it. Same thing with your copy. You need to fully convince your perfect prospect that the next step will be in full alignment with their journey and will support them with getting to their end goal.

So think back to copy you've written before, are you selling a webinar or a lead magnet before the webinar?

Pay attention, stay precise and you'll do great!

CHAPTER 8
THE MOST IMPORTANT PIECE OF THE PUZZLE

You must know by now, (or maybe you don't) that marketers and copywriters, including myself, do their best to withhold the greatest tips, tricks and hacks that really push the needle over the edge.

That's why we can claim to be apart of that all so exclusive 1% club. You know where the wealthiest 1% of the world owns more wealth than the bottom 90% combined.[2]

If we gave up these precious secrets would we remain the top 1% or would the competition continue to grow and grow and grow?

Well the truth is, at least in my eyes, that even if we gave everyone the same amount of money to start with the rich would get it back and the poor would remain poor anyways.

Even if we gave them all the same knowledge.

Why?

Because the knowledge is readily accessible to anyone and everyone. It comes down to the desire to become great. And that leads me into why I'm writing about this particular topic right this second.

You're reading this because you're either a 1%er and know without a shred of a doubt that the more knowledge you possess the greater chances of keeping and growing your wealth will be.

OR

You're not a 1%er... yet. You're on your way and you're trying to really understand what it takes to make it into that club. For you it may not be about the money, but the impact you can leave on the world. Some people volunteer their time, other donate 100's of millions of dollars building schools, housing and other resources across the world helping millions and millions of people.

I know for me and the impact I want to leave on this world I need to be a 1%er and that's why I've gone through my go through and hustled my way to where I am. I've invested tens if not hundreds of thousands of dollars on personal development, coaches and courses. I have to tell you...

The return on investment (ROI) on that is nothing short of 10 fold. Even 100 fold.

So my thought is this:

If I can impact 1 million people with this book and each of them can impact 1 million people...

I've just "hacked" donating and charitable cause by the truck load.

By giving you this new skill set of copywriting and helping you get your message and your clients message into millions and millions of peoples hands across the world... I am able to claim a small piece of that victory for both of us.

So with that being said...

...I have to give you my best stuff.
No fluff, no holding back and certainly
no beating around the bush.

This chapter is going to dive deep into one of the most important pieces to not just writing copy, but how to position your business or company into the marketplace for EXTREME growth.

Without this chapter you would be lost, unclear and completely guessing about how to approach scaling.

Whether you're a complete newbie or a Fortune 500 executive, this book will positively impact the way you run your business and life.

So let's dive in, shall we?

This chapter is fully dedicated to knowing your customer, industry, brand, business and life inside and out.

Can you guess what I'm talking about yet?

If not don't worry... I'll give you the answer momentarily.

For now let me tease at it and really test how patient you are before you skip ahead. (trust me, you'll want to stick this out and read every single word to really grasp this full concept)

Having a crisp and clear understanding of your customer is crucial.

Here's why:

If you know who your perfect prospect is, you'll know exactly what to sell them. You don't want to offer up a mini-van to a 16 year old guy do you?

Of course there are rare occasions where that might actually be a good fit, but how would you know that unless you know who your perfect prospect is?

But here's an even more important piece to the puzzle... when you know who your perfect prospect is, you'll know HOW to sell them.

That's right, your perfect prospect will tell you exactly how to sell them.

On the other hand, the same will go for your industry, brand, business and life.

Have you guessed what this chapter is about yet?

Well...

I guess I can spill the metaphorical beans now right?

I'm going to break down the exact methods I use to conduct my high level, FBI equivalent and detective like research to bring out the language, verbiage, tonality and triggers that get perfect prospects begging to hand over their hard earned cash for whatever it is you may be selling to them.

Research is truly what makes the world go round. Back in the old days we would have to go out and knock on doors and ask people questions and write down their answers. (I say that as if I've been in the marketing space since 1990 LOL)

With technology and everything going on... it's just super easy.

We can fire up our laptops or smartphones (that are already fired up) and simply blast out a quick poll asking people this or that. We can receive the answers in minutes compared to the old days where it would take us weeks.

So over the next few minutes or so I'll be breaking down how I conduct my research. I know I've said it before, but you're really going to want to consume EVERY single word that you read from here until the back cover of this book.

So my research comes down into 3 phases.

- Phase 1: Perfect Prospect (Who)
- Phase 2: Hangout Spots (Where)
- Phase 3: Verbiage, Triggers (How)

Each phase is just as important as the next and without all three phases combined in unison there is no question you will not succeed to the highest level possible.

So I beg with you.

Do **<u>NOT</u>** cut corners.

Phase 1: Perfect Prospect

Think of yourself as the architect constructing the
John Hancock building in downtown Chicago. You
know, the one that Opera once lived in.

Anyways,

That building at one point in time stood amongst
the tallest buildings in the entire world. Building
such a marvelous building requires precise
measurements and planning.

You're going to construct your perfect prospect
with that same precise measurement and
planning.

The good news is that you won't have to guess
what the blueprint looks like. I'm going to lay it all
out for you as clear and precise as possible.

All you have to do?

Fill in the blanks.

Ready?

Set?

GO!

Kidding, this isn't a race. Take your time. (I've just always wanted to do that in a book, and that was my chance)

So here's how you construct your perfect prospect:

You can download a FREE Perfect Prospect template at

https://writelikethewolf.com/perfectprospect

The template will give you EVERYTHING you need to construct your perfect prospect.

The next few paragraphs will be tough if you don't have the guide right in front of you, so I'd definitely recommend to bookmark this page and download that Template for FREE.

Now that you have your Perfect Prospect Template in hand here's what you'll do with it:

At the very top you'll write down or type your product or service. This will hopefully implant this into your subconscious so you're making decisions based upon your product.

You'll notice the very first question asks for age.

Now there is no right or wrong answers for any of these.

Just remember that no one offers a product or service that fits everyone's life no matter how hard you try to manipulate it to fit.

Your product/service has a very specific customer that NEEDS it.

Your age range should never vary more than 7 years and even that is pushing it.

Here's why:

Think of this for a second, what was your priority in life when you were 20? Graduate college or maybe level up in your career?

Think of when you were 27... were you trying to start a family and buy your second home?

You see... life changes drastically over a 7 year period. Your product or service DOES NOT FIT that big of a range of people.

I recommend 3-5 year age range here. This will generate you THE BEST results possible. (most of the time.)

The next question asks for gender.

If you follow me at all you know one of my good friends is Nikolas Elliot. He's currently the VP of Sales for Lady Boss Fitness phone team. One of the leading fitness brands in the world ranking #19 on the Inc. 500 list.

So their perfect prospect's gender would be female. Right?

Of course.

So if your product or service is going to be sold to a specific gender... it's good to know that up front. Women and men both speak and receive information differently. This will make more sense during the next phases of research.

Now the third, fourth and maybe even fifth part of the perfect prospect equation is their interests.

Instead of just filling out a bunch of stuff randomly let me give you the specifics you need to be paying attention to here.

You need to single out hobbies, celebrities they follow, people they look up to, religion (if applicable), books they read, authors they follow, Social Media pages they like... etc.

Get as specific as you can here. Do not hold back, the more information you gather the more specific you can get.

The final piece of the Perfect Prospect Template is going to cover income.

How much money do they make?

Get specific here. Are you helping business owners generating 7 figures who are stuck? Or are you helping bridge the gap from $300,000/yr to earn their first $1,000,000?

You cannot and will not help a $50k per year earner the same way you will help a $5,000,000 per year earner. It's simply not possible. They will need support and inspiration in different ways.

GET SPECIFIC. (if you're not sure... reevaluate your offerings.)

Now that you have your Perfect Prospect Template filled out with all of your own information you'll be able to move on to the next phase.

Phase 2: Hangout Spots

This one isn't going to be as in-depth as the previous phase.

Here's why:

There are only a few places your prospects can hangout.

Either online or offline.

The good news is that Social Media will bring in over 2.77 Billion ACTIVE Users in 2019.[8] Depending on when you're reading this book, it may be a heck of a lot more than that.

If we took the ole MLM Approach... and just had to sell 1% of that market... that is still 27,000,000 people. If you sold each of these people something for $1.00 every year... well that'd be an 8 figure business without even trying.

So there is a VERY good chance that your Perfect Prospect is hanging out on Social Media nearly every single day.

So for the sake of... forget it. We're going to focus on the online section because if you don't, you're simply trying to self-sabotage your own success.

Your Perfect Prospect is basically guaranteed to hangout on Social Media.

So...

...*here we go!*

I'm about to break down exactly how to find your Perfect Prospect on social media in less than 2 minutes.

Seems impossible right?

Wrong.

I can assume that you still have your template in front of you... right?

Again if you didn't download the Perfect Prospect Template go to

https://writelikethewolf.com/perfectprospect

So let's focus on the interests category.

Pick one of their interests. It could be watches or it could simply be coaching, public speaking, coffee, cats, dogs, dating, books... etc. Whatever it may be that's okay just pick one for now.

Pull up your Facebook account.

** DISCLAIMER**

This book is not a part of the Facebook website or Facebook Inc. Additionally, This book is NOT endorsed by Facebook in any way.
FACEBOOK is a trademark of FACEBOOK, Inc.

Alright now that you're on your Facebook account you'll want to use the search bar.

Choose one of the interests that you have written down on your Perfect Prospect Template. Type that interest into the search bar and find a group that is associated with it.

You have now infiltrated the top secret off the map hangout spot for your perfect customer where they are the most vulnerable.

Phase 3: Anti-Selling

Here's the most important piece of the puzzle...

...are you ready?

I doubt it.

But I'm going to tell you anyways.

DO NOT SELL THEM ANYTHING.

Don't do it. Don't pitch them. Don't get them on your list. Don't get them on the phone. Just observe. Study them.

Here's what I do in order:

- I scroll and take notes on what questions are being brought up and how often
- I scroll and take notes on what problems I see them having that they don't know they have
- I take those notes and begin piecing together how my product/solution is a DIRECT solution to their problem

Sounds easy right?

It is.

DO NOT COMPLICATE THIS.

Now that you have a good idea of what they're going through and how they perceive their reality it's time to do some intentional searching.

Inside of the group there will be a search bar. Now you can type in some keywords from your notes and organize all the posts together.

You can begin either asking more questions or helping answer some questions inside of the group itself. This will open up direct communication with your Perfect Prospect.

REMINDER!
DO NOT SELL THEM ANYTHING!

You're simply gathering information right now. That one sale will not make or break you... and if it will you need to see the bigger picture here.

You're gathering trigger words and can even begin testing out ideas in conversations. Do not sell them anything, but simply conduct this as a "survey" or "interview."

You can grab a set of example survey and interview questions here:

https://writelikethewolf.com/surveyquestions

You'll set this information aside and then apply it as you learn what this book will teach you.

If social media isn't available to you... *don't worry*

If you've looked into copywriting at all you've probably stumbled upon the name Gary Halbert more than once.

He was one of the best direct response copywriters to ever walk the earth and it was rumored and believed to be very true that Gary would go to the bar and chat with people or even knock doors to get the information he needed. Don't be afraid of taking the old school approach if other resources aren't available.

Start getting fired up for the next chapter where we will be discussing how to choose the right approach to your copy.

I'll see you on the next page.

CHAPTER 9
CHOOSING THE
RIGHT APPROACH

This chapter is about to absolutely annihilate everything the guru's, experts and influencers tell you about the world.

Regardless of what you've heard, read or seen in some video or funnel or webinar...

> *...there is more than one*
> *approach to do everything.*

Choosing the right approach to start with so you don't light money on fire and run around with your head cut off?

That can be a bit tricky... well it was before I decided to write this chapter.

So you're in luck! Woo hoo. This is your "win" for today.

So buckle up, you're going for a ride.

Alright,

Now that I've made a really big promise of delivering you what no other guru, influencer or expert has set out to deliver I guess I have to start making good on it.

Choosing the proper approach can make or break most marketing campaigns.

There are more than a dozen different types of approaches, but some of them share a rooted cause for choosing them.

A lot like a tree.

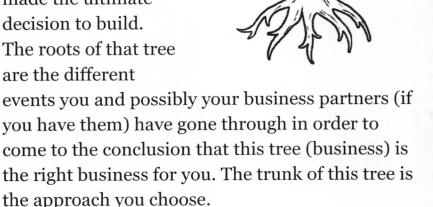

The tree as a whole is the evolutionary business that you've made the ultimate decision to build. The roots of that tree are the different events you and possibly your business partners (if you have them) have gone through in order to come to the conclusion that this tree (business) is the right business for you. The trunk of this tree is the approach you choose.

I like to take a minute to paint you a visual of what that actually represents. In my life time I have seen tens or even hundreds of thousands of trees. From the pacific northwest evergreens, to the midwest's apple trees, all the way to the coast of California palm trees. I've seen them all.

The biggest thing to note is that a good amount of these trees were similar to one another. I would see a tree in the midwest and go "that's a pacific northwest tree." And I know what you're thinking at this exact moment. You're probably thinking "what the hell do trees have to do with writing copy?"

To be completely transparent with you...

...*nothing and everything at the same time.*

There are certain types of trees and for the most part they look the same and the "type" they're identified as.

These "types" are the approaches you'll be choosing for your copy. Each type of tree serves its purpose.

When you choose your approach you're essentially choosing the type of business you'll be operating. The business plan, marketing plan, fulfillment plan and scaling plan will all be rooted from the initial approach you choose.

"But what if I choose the wrong approach?"

A question I've included due to the sole purpose of it being the very next thought that will pop into your head.

You can't choose the wrong approach if you stay true to the data. If you remain objective and follow the numbers you have a strong chance at choosing the right approach from the get go.

For those of you who do not have a single shred of data to look at, well, you'll need to choose an approach with the end in mind.

Here's what I mean by that:

When you choose an approach it's the entry point for a customer to walk into your world. However, don't get stuck on where the initial "impact" may be. Instead, I'd like to suggest that you take a look at the start to finish process for that customer initially walking into your world through that particular approach you're choosing.

What's the next step? And the next one and next one and next one... so on and so forth until the end of time.

Do this with every single approach until you can look and go "that one objectively makes the most sense!"

For those of you who make decisions like I do... quick, fast and based on logic then you'll be able to see the end of these approaches and the middle and pick one almost instantly. Don't be afraid to pivot later on... but trust your gut. Believe me, it will work for you as it has for me and everyone I've coached on this.

Still not sure which type you are? That's completely okay. You're what we call "special" and I mean that in the best way possible. You most likely analyze a situation until you receive the logic necessary. Sometimes you have questions, sometimes you don't. Either way you look exploring multiple routes before committing. This is completely okay. In fact, sometimes I make my decisions just like this.

Go through one by one until you see one that you keep comparing everything to. Once you have the one constant, that's the approach that you're attached to for whatever reason. Run with it.

Alright, so enough about how to choose the right approach. Let's dive into what these approaches are, so you have a clear understanding of who, what, where, when, why and how.

Fair Enough?

The 3 Approaches To Writing Pretty Darn Good Copy That Converts ~~ALL of the time~~ most of the time

CEO Copy

When you're writing CEO Copy you're stepping out from behind your PR team or business itself and becoming open and honest with what's going on. This can allow an authoritative approach when crafted properly. Think along the lines of "leading from the front" rather than pointing fingers and asking why this and that isn't what you wanted it to be.

This approach can be done even if you're not a massive CEO or a CEO at all. The name of this

approach is simply derived from the tonality and prescription when writing this.

I'd refer you to read letters to shareholders from some of the greatest CEO's of the world. For an incredible example of letters to shareholders I would suggest Amazon's annual letters from CEO Jeff Bezo's.

You can find them for free here:

http://bit.ly/amazonletters

You'll see the style and I have high hopes that you'll take this style and apply it if you feel this approach is a good approach for you and your business.

Long Form

As I'm sure you've figured out... long form is simply very long sales copy. This will consist of pulling emotions and backing it up with logic

before finally revealing what it is that you're trying to offer them.

Some of the best long form examples will be found on Agora Financial's website. They have some of the highest quality and fine tuned copy ever released and it's all extremely long form.

This is often considered as a demonstration ad where you virtually place your product or service into their hand and begin to demonstrate the benefits before yanking it out of their hands and asking them to buy.

This is especially effective with physical products!

Story Telling

This is probably the more common of all of the types that is used and for a good reason too. You see, as humans we love stories and they've been around since the beginning of time.

Stories allow for emotions to pour out and for readers to get sucked in... when done properly. Storytelling is powerful.

You can tell the story of your old uncle rick and how he stumbled at work and it cost him nearly 6 months of pay until he discovered he signed up for this incredible disability insurance that paid 150% of his normal pay...

> *... if you're selling life insurance you have now shown proof through story telling that your product BENEFITS your customer.*

This will make them reach for their wallet to hand you money don't you think?

Now, these are the three most common approaches that I use. Can you do some digging and find more approaches? Sure. Are they as effective? My data would tell me no, but that doesn't mean you shouldn't test them out. Remember, my data and your data will most likely look different. Your key to success here is to test!

So when you're choosing an approach to your copy, think of your perfect prospect and how they would want to be sold.

So now knowing what the 3 best approaches are based off my own personal results and how you can apply them... how do you determine the best one?

Well, for the experts that are reading this right now that are generating millions upon millions of dollars of revenue through copy already know this answer.

For those of you who may be new to the game I'll explain this as simple as I can so you can really take in all that I'm about to share with you.

It's two words that true expert marketers LOVE and fake guru's HATE.

Split-Test.

That's right. Want to discover the BEST approach?
Test multiple. Because without the data truly
telling you which one will perform better, you're
doing nothing more than guessing at what the
"best" one is.

You deserve better than that.

Test test test.

Even after spitting out over 1,000,000 words (and
honestly, by the time you're reading this book it's
probably closer to double that) The only thing I
can tell you with confidence is that there are
many, many, many approaches and even more
"styles" and "voices." The best thing to do is find
one of these approaches, apply them in your own
style & voice and test test test.

There's a strong belief inside of me that each of us
are unique. We're built unique. We're raised
unique. We think unique. We are simply unique.

This means that there is a rule. What works for me, may not work for you.

The good news is? One of these three approaches will work for you. If you've dialed in your audience and mapped out your plan... the approach you take with your copy will fall into its proper place.

SECTION FOUR
HOW TO . . .

Chapter 10
Get MORE Clicks in
5 Minutes or Less

Getting clicks can mean a whole lot of different things, but for the sake of this chapter we will be talking about getting a click that progresses the sale further and further along.

This is truly the start of your entire online business. Without a click you simply can't generate a lead or close a sale. Think about it, how does someone get to your website? They click on your link. They click search on google. They click on your ad. They click on something. And to prevent any of my sarcastics friends from making a comment about it... yes they can swipe up on social media too which also counts as a click.

So how hard could it be to get someone to click?

A recent Forbes articles stated that we are subject to nearly 10,000 advertisements PER DAY.[3]

So you only have to fight 10,000 other people every single day for that click. Depending on how many ads you click on per day you would be 3 times more likely to play in the NBA after High School than you are to get a click and 9 times more likely to play in the NFL. (3 in 10,000 make it to the NBA, 9 in 10,000 make it to the NFL)[4]

So knowing that the odds are stacked against you, would you like a look at how to stack them back in your favor? If yes, keep reading. If no, throw this book away or donate to someone in need.

This chapter is all about how to get someone to click.

Now before we really begin into what makes people click and how to actually get them to click, we must understand WHY someone will click.

One of the exercises I have all of my students complete inside of Write Like The Wolf Academy is to think about why they personally would click on an ad.

What makes you click? Is it the headline? Image? Subheadline?

What about that headlines, image or subheadline? Is it curiosity? Do they have a similarities?

Now regardless of what these answers might actually look like for you let's break down some of the most heavily clicked ads in the history of the world and see if we can spot a common theme amongst them that we can apply to our own products and services.

Sound good?

Free Book Reveals How To Create Internet Campaigns That *Sell.*

From The Desk Of Frank Kern
La Jolla, Ca.
February 2014

Dear Friend,

If you'd like to create Internet campaigns that sell like crazy ...regardless of your industry, this is the most important book you'll ever read.

And by the way,

Let's focus on the Headline.[5]

"FREE BOOK REVEALS
How To Create Internet
Campaigns That Sell"

Let's create our formula:

How To Create
_____ That Sell

How To *do this thing*
That *insert desired result*

So I'll create a real estate example using our new templates.

How to Create
Listings That *Sell!*

And I'll use the next template to create an engaging headline that gets clicks for a marshmallow gun.

How To *Build A Marshmallow Gun* That *Is Slightly Dangerous* But *Wildly Fun*

The idea is that you want to create curiosity. Humans by nature want to learn and uncover more stuff. If I can use these templates and apply them to a marshmallow gun business to generate clicks... then you can certainly apply these same techniques to any business, any industry and any products or service in the world.

The question is how will you apply it?

Now instead of using up the exact same eye popping template every single time you write anything to get a click let's walk through my exact process for creating these from scratch.

Sound good?

This process is called the "cliffhanger" effect. Remember when you would watch some type of action or suspense filled T.V. show before you could skip the ads?

Think of how they end each small segment before going to a commercial break. They build the suspense all the way up and leave you begging for more while you're stuck having to watch the commercials before they reveal what happens next.

It's the perfect template/mindset to get into.

So what are some examples you can model for your own?

You'll never believe what (testimonial persons name) did before (result)...

How To (get what they want) Without Having To (common pain)

So here's an example of using the first template for an ad agency that wants to generate more leads for themselves.

**You'll Never Believe What
This _Contractor_ Did Before
Becoming A Millionaire**

And here's an example of the second template for the health/fitness niche.

How To Get *Washboard Abs* WITHOUT *Doing A SINGLE SIT-UP*

The biggest key factor here is to zone in and get specific. At first it may seem like you need a lot of words to get the message across. You need to condense it to 12 words or less. Ideally you'll want to shoot for 8, but I know this isn't always possible.

Now that you have a few samples of building your own templates I want to show you where you can go out and find samples of your own. You know, like if you did 5 minutes of research kind of thing.

So first and foremost you can find great examples of advertising and copywriting at swiped.co. This is a collection of some of the highest converting ads written by some of the best in marketing. You'll often find some old ads dated from the early 1950s and earlier. Which is okay because some of the ideas that worked back then still work today.

So all of this chapter has been strictly dedicated to helping you get more clicks, but honestly this chapter has done a whole lot more than that. We really focused on building out highly clicked on headlines. Be sure to mark this chapter as we will be referencing the templates and template creation discussed inside of this chapter to help us with the rest of the book.

Simply put:

Headlines ARE IMPORTANT.

The late Gary Halbert was quoted saying that the Headline can be responsible for up to 85% of the buying decision.

And think about it...

I created a mental click from you on this chapter right?

I titled this section "How To ...."

And this chapter is titled "Get MORE Clicks in 5 Minutes or Less"

I used the same templates discussed in this chapter to get you to "click" in your mind that you need to read this chapter. In fact, I have a sneaky suspicion that some of you reading this right now skipped the rest of the book and jumped straight into this chapter.

If that is you, I'm sorry but...

Go back to page one and start reading from there. I don't care what guru told you to skip around and pick out the good info from books and apply it. This book isn't some "FREE + Shipping" funnel piece that was written specifically to indoctrinate you into my Wolf Pack.

This book was strictly written to take you from where you're at to where you need to go inside of 228 pages. If you follow the process from page 1 all the way until the back cover your chances of success significantly increase.

Although I'm glad that my chapter title intrigued you enough to skip half of the book, I strongly suggest starting from page 1.

CHAPTER 11
WRITE A WILDLY
PROFITABLE SALES LETTER

I have a sneaky suspicion that the reason most 8-figure marketers are earning 8-figures or more annually is because they've set up their sales letters to actually sell rather than be a source of information.

Where on earth does this suspicion come from? Well, I've seen tens of thousands of sales letters and have even written a good amount myself, but the ones that truly stand out are sales letters that continue to sell all the way from start to finish.

So what does that mean for you?

A few things actually:

- You Shouldn't Pay $50 For Someone To Write Your Sales Letter For You
- You Need A Dialed In Process For Writing Your Sales Letter
- You Need To Know Your Intention Behind Your Sales Letter

Now, I certainly hope the first one is understood and I don't have to go into great detail to explain it. But just because I know there is some "guru" out there right now going "the Sales Letter doesn't matter just throw someone a few bucks and move on to the important stuff." I have to explain a little more in depth.

If you're a copywriter as you read this you'll be screaming at the top of your lungs "YES YES YES YES AMEN HALLELUJAH" and for marketers and entrepreneurs not familiar with how copywriters actually earn a living... you're in for a treat.

First some context.

A Sales Letter needs to be as long as it needs to be. It could be as short as a 700 words or a 20,000 word letter.. Regardless of what's going on your Sales Letter should be set up to selling your new lead on the next step of your process.

So here's an example:

Let's say you sell a course for $10,000 through a coaching call.

Your funnel looks like this:

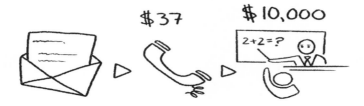

Sales Letter | Sales Call | Coaching Program

I'm not saying this is the only way or how simple this can actually be, I'm just using an example from one of my current clients.

So your Sales Letter in this event is selling people on signing up for your $37 coaching call that is designed to sell your $10,000 coaching program.

Most marketers or copywriter or even entrepreneurs (coaches in this situation) would look at this and say that the coaching call is worth $37. An A-List copywriter looks at that coaching call and understands the value of that coaching call is well over $100,000.

Here's why...

That phone call you're selling from your sales letter is an opportunity for that prospect to (hopefully) add an additional 6 or 7 figures to their annual revenue. Why do I say this? Because your $10,000 coaching program needs to be justified by the results it brings. In most cases especially the successful ones you'll notice that the cost of a program is 1/10th of the expected results at the minimum.

So if it's a $10,000 program your average client should be adding $100,000 in results from your program.

So that coaching call you're selling is essentially worth $100,000 at the minimum. So you need to sell it as such. Not as if it's just an easy way to get qualified people on the phone that pay you to be a lead.

This is why one of the biggest lessons I teach my students is to begin with the end in mind. It can be really tough to write an ad if you don't know what the landing page is supposed to do... and so on and so forth. Make sense?

As you continue to read every word in this chapter you'll soon uncover exactly what your Sales Letter should look like from start to finish. This will give you the ability to make some changes to your current sales letter or even start from scratch if you've never writing a sales letter before.

Let's dive in shall we?

So this is the framework you'll use and can even fill in the blanks.

Step 1: Attractive Headline

An attractive headline will consist of anything and everything that can get someone hooked into what you're about to share with them. For easy reference jump back to the chapter before this one to see some examples and templates of headlines that work. Think of this as your mental "click" that sucks your reader in and forces their brain to beg for more. Kind of like baiting a fishing line.

Step 2: Intro

This is what I call the hook for the bait. If you've ever been fishing you know that when you cast your line out into the water it has a hook on it. That hook is meaningless without any bait. Your Attractive Headline is your bait in this situation. That bait will get a fish hooked on your line, but to keep them hooked you have to yank your hook into place. That's what the intro does.

You see you'll catch someone's attention and get them to stop, but it's what you say next that will determine if they'll continue listening or not. That's what our intro does for us!

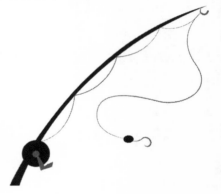

Step 3: Back Story

This is where you'll begin to tell your story. Remember, stories sell if you don't ramble too much and they have a good structure. Your goal here is simply to sell them on the fact that you were once exactly like them. They should feel as if they wrote this part of the story themselves.

I hate that I even have to bring this up and it's most likely not a reminder for you, but maybe for someone you know. Do not make this story up. The power in copy is from the vulnerability and truth that you'll pour onto paper. If you don't have a story go and find someone that has this story that you need to tell and tell it from their perspective.

This is the part where you cast your line into the water.

Step 4: Turning Point

The turning point is exactly what it sounds like. This is where you no longer have to suffer with the pain and agony of whatever the true pain of your perfect avatar is. You have discovered a new way and you made the decision to push forward with it.

This is the first part of your sales letter where they will actually start to see your offer a little bit.

Kind of like when the fish is starting to nibble or run into your line. You begin to yank on the line a little bit to catch the fish.

Step 5: Benefits, Testimonials, Bullets

Talking about the benefits, not the facts will get your readers over the edge. Reading or watching about how someone else got the results they want can push someone over the edge.

You can combine both of these and create bullets or add bullets after the fact. Either way this lethal combo will have your conversions sky rocketing.

This is where the fish is officially caught and on your line. All of your "selling and work" is complete.

Step 6: Call To Action

If you don't tell them what to do next they'll never do it. People can't always put two and two together. So help them do it.

"If you want results just like Bob is getting every single month, then click the button below to book your exclusive 1 on 1 coaching call."

It can be that simple.

This is where you reel in that fish and start heading back to shore!

So now that you have your new sales letter frame work are you going to apply it?

Can you see how this will impact your business for the better?

** Mini bonus **

You should be using this exact framework to write your lead magnets as well. For instance:

If you're giving away a FREE eBook as your front end offer, make your eBook a sales letter. It's that easy.

CHAPTER 12
WRITE VSL'S

I have no idea what year you're reading this book in. It could be 2019, 2050 or even the year 3000. Regardless, I believe that video is here to stay.

As I'm writing this we are in a huge transitional period from extremely long copy to video with a transcript of the video.

For those of you that recognize this transition or simply the importance of pouring some extremely powerful words into a video script, this chapter is FOR YOU.

Over the next few pages you'll uncover exactly how to craft some of the ugliest, but highest converting video scripts the world will ever see.

So like anything we must step into why the market has shifted from 30, 40 and even 50 page sales letters to 20, 30 and 45 minute video sales letters.

You'll soon notice if you haven't already that good copy has everything to do with psychology and nothing to do with "sales."

Our attention span is becoming smaller and smaller all the while distractions are increasing at an alarming rate.

Videos, ads, pop ups, video games, notifications and essentially the entire world at our fingertips it's nearly impossible to keep anyones attention for more than a few seconds.

This is when my resourcefulness came into play in a huge way. You see, most people would have to spend thousands, millions or even more to receive the type of research that I've sneakily acquired for our benefit.

Here's what I found after acquiring this research...

...video sales letters are selling at an alarming rate.

I'm not sure where at in the world you are or what type of resources you have at your disposal, but when you look at some industry letters in direct response marketing like Agora or the leaders on sites like ClickBank and JV Zoo, you'll notice a trend amongst the "winners."

That trend is video sales letters. Not just any sales letters, but extremely powerful and persuasive video sales letters that have a very consistent framework that I'm about to share with you here.

Sounds almost too good to be true right? I mean Agora is doing nearly $1 Billion (with a B) in annual revenue from direct response marketing. ClickBank and JV Zoo are some of the top sites for affiliate marketers to find high converting products. Some of these products have sold over 113,000 customers in just a short time frame.

Could you imagine what 113,000 customers could do for you or your business?

Leveraging a video sales letter is crucial and I want to break down their framework for you here so you can easily duplicate the same structure and plug in your own story, product or service.

So be prepared for your mind to be BLOWN.

Step 1: Open With A Shocking Statement

I'm not sure if this will come as a surprise to you or not, but if you can absolutely shock someone with something that they believe has a small possibility of being true you have a very great chance of keeping their attention.

Here's an example:

"$46 Billion Was Made Yesterday. Is It Yours?"

It's pretty bold and shocking right? How could someone make $46 Billion in a single day? Is it even possible? What would happen if I did that? What would I buy first?

So many questions come to mind and that is exactly what you want your perfect prospect to feel.

Step 2: Introduce The Problem

In this step you'll want to introduce the problem and show them why it's the most significant problem in their life right now.

You'll want to focus on just one problem. So think of it from a 10,000 foot view.

Here's what I mean:

The problem might be that they aren't making money. But the solution you offer is lead generation. So the problem you'll want to focus on is not that they aren't making enough money, but that they aren't generating enough leads.

Here's an example:

"Have you doubled your income year over year? If not, this video is for you. If you're anything like our clients and I have a pretty good feeling you are, then you're not bad at what you do, you just don't have enough qualified leads to talk to!"

Step 3: Irritate The Problem

This is where most copywriters, entrepreneurs and marketers miss the mark. They have incredible copy, but forget to irritate the problem enough to the point everyone who should buy, does.

Here's why most of us don't do this. It makes our prospects uncomfortable. It could upset them and even make them angry. But at the end of the day when you receive good advice from someone even though it isn't what you wanted to hear, you look back and thank them for it because it made you better. (even if you didn't tell them)

So dig and dig and dig until you think you're being annoying about it and then you should dig some more.

Step 4: Go DEEPER

This is the most important step. Right when you thought you dug as deep as you could, how could you twist the pain just a little bit more to push them over the edge?

This is where you're going to watch the dominos fall. This is where your sales are going to come from. And this is where A-List copywriters make a name for themselves.

One of the 8 reasons people buy is to reduce pain. When you continue to raise the level of pain they feel due to the problem you introduced that they relate to you'll begin to see people making the decision to improve their lives.

It's your responsibility as Uncle G would say.

Step 5: Introduce The Solution

This is where the offer will begin to peak through. This could be the "aha" moment or the turning point in the story. Whatever it is, this is the light at the end of the tunnel and the offer you're about to make is the car that is going to get them to their destination and beyond.

Step 6: Credibility

Who are you and why should they listen to you?

And as I'm writing this I realized that there is a secret that most people don't know about this credibility thing that I feel I must share with you...

> *...stop putting yourself on a pedestal here. You're not credible on video because you're featured in Forbes.*

You're credible because you were once where they are feeling their pain and now you've implemented the solution to the pain and no longer have to deal with it.

This is why people believe you're credible.

Step 7: Proof!

I think this goes without saying, but do not fabricate this. If you have yet to get results for someone just go out and offer whatever it is you're offering for FREE for a few people until you have solid results you can insert.

Proof of concept by ordinary people is great. Remember, you don't want David Goggins to be your proof for losing weight. You want some ordinary person no one has heard of with incredible before and after photos.

Step 8: Stack

This is where you'll lay out EXACTLY what they'll be getting. Line by line. Item by item. Value by value. This works best when used with bullet points.

Attached a value to each bullet point.

When you add up all of your stack it should equal 10x what your asking price is.

Step 9: Urgency

Do not use some BS reason on why they should by now.

Don't: "I'm taking this offer down in 48 hours because I simply can't fulfill the demand"

Do: "I'm not sure how long this will be available as we are already shipping at full capacity! So act now to avoid being placed on the back order list!"

Give them a REAL and SPECIFIC reason as to why they should buy now. If you don't have a reason they should... create one and make it genuine.

Step 10: CLOSE CLOSE CLOSE!

This is my favorite part of sales, business and life in general. Getting what you want because you asked for it.

Example " Buy My Stuff Now!"

The idea is that you need to ask for the sale.

Tell them how to buy what you're selling.

Example: "Click The Link Below & Finish Your Order!"

Do not forget this step as simple as it may seem, most people have no clue what to do after they watch a presentation. So help them out a little here why don't ya?

Now that I've laid this out as simple as it could possibly be, you're all set to go.

Make sure you utilize each step in the proper order to get insane results for your next VSL you write!

CHAPTER 13
WRITE WILDLY PROFITABLE
WEBINAR SCRIPTS

Make no mistake, there are two different types of webinars.

Wildly Profitable Webinars.

AND

Wildly Catastrophic Webinars.

If you happened to read the title of this chapter then you know we'll be focusing on the Wildly Profitable Webinars. However, I wanted to dig a bit deeper than most people do when discussing how to create your webinar.

So this chapter will be quite long, but jam packed with everything you'll need to craft a Wildly Profitable Webinar Script from scratch for any industry selling any product or service at any price point.

There are a few basic steps that you'll follow with some intense deep dives into what each step actually entails and how to execute it flawlessly.

Step 1: Intro
Step 2: Story
Step 3: Trial Close
Step 4: Close
Step 5: Close Some More

Now,

The framework will remain the same regardless of who you are and what you sell. What changes is the content inside of each of these steps.

So over the next few minutes you'll uncover exactly how to write out an intro, story, trial close, close and most importantly, the additional closing needed.

Step 1: Intro

I remember back to some of the first webinars I ever watched on the back end and was thinking "what the hell are they even talking about right now?"

These were some of the webinars that fueled this desire to test some strong webinar intros to not only hook people in to what you're about to pitch them over the next 45 to 90 minutes, but to truthfully set the stage for how well your offer converts at the end.

The results of these tests would absolutely blow your mind... if I could share with you the stats. However, I can't and even if I did I don't think you'd believe me anyways.

The good thing is that if you follow this Webinar intro process you'll have a great deal of success and your own results will fuel your need to share this with everyone you know or to keep it to yourself. However you intend on leveraging this information is completely up to you.

Inside of every introduction there are 5 very important pieces that need to be addressed.

1.   Expectations
2.   Why They Should Stay On
3.   Command Authority
4.   Qualify Yourself
5.   Pacing

Setting expectations upfront is key. Over 40,000,000 Americans suffer from anxiety that we know about.[6] Some of the biggest drivers of anxiety comes from the unknown. What's about to happen and when.

So why not put your attendees at ease by letting them know exactly what to expect?

If you don't give them a good reason to stay you may lose them. Remember the average human has a shorter attention span than a goldfish. Give them an incentive to stay on. You could give out a webinar handbook, free mini course, merch... anything. Give them a good reason to stay on.

Webinars are basically a group hangout with a chat box. There are usually a bunch of people attending these (or at least you hope) and getting a group of people to sit down, pay attention and not disrupt you is challenging. Command authority up front and let them know you're running the show. They'll be okay with this. I know it'll feel uncomfortable at first, but it's needed.

Qualify yourself in such a way that has your audience believing you are the answer to their prayers. This means that you've once lives their life and now live their dream life. I've said this before and I'll continue to say it...

DO NOT LIE.

This part is not your entire life story. It's a simple: "If you're not familiar with who I am I'll take a quick moment to introduce myself. I'm Cole VanDeWoestyne and not long ago I was working 100+ hours a week at multiple jobs making someone else rich before I said Fuck this, I'm out and became one of the top copywriters in the internet marketing world writing for some of the most famous and influential marketers in the game today producing over 8-figures in results directly tied to my words."

This ties directly into setting the pace up. So here's what setting the pace looks like... "And over the next 90 minutes I'll be taking you along my journey and how I was able to craft words that have turned into 10's of millions of dollars in just 12 months with no previous experience, connections or clue what I was doing. I do talk a little fast, but will be having a full on Q&A at the end of this where you can ask me questions, so be sure to write them down!"

If you craft your intro properly you'll be able to not only capture their attention, but have them already curious about how they can learn more from you and even pay you to help them get to where they want to go and they don't even know you have an offer yet.

Some things to keep in mind:

Stories do sell. If you don't have an interesting story, you should be finding one that you can tell. I'll give you a great example of how this was done to generate $3.2 Million in just 90 minutes.

You can slide a relatable story to bridge into the story you're about to tell.

If you're unsure of what I'm talking about well, you're in for a treat. I still get goosebumps watching this presentation happen.

Russell Brunson the founder of ClickFunnels gave a 90 minute presentation at Grant Cardone's 10X Growth Con in 2018 and generated over $3.2 Million in sales from the stage. He started with not his story, but the story of Roger Bannister. Roger Bannister was a sprinter back in the 1960's and he broke the first 4 minute mile. He goes on and on talking about how no one thought it was possible until he did it. Then everyone started to do it.

He bridged the gap between Roger Bannister's story and Step: 2 of our webinar script process.

Step 2: Story

Don't forget Chapter Seven where we discussed The One Thing. This is important for you to remember when writing anything, but especially a Wildly Profitable Webinar Script.

Your goal during this step in the process is to sell them on one thing. You'll be taking them through a single journey with three big parts.

Part 1: New Vehicle (new opportunity)
Part 2: Their Ability To Use The Vehicle (internal beliefs)
Part 3: Eliminate Doubt (the 1 thing keeping them from doing it)

For each of these parts you'll need a story that relates to the goal of the part. So for instance, you'll have to tell a story about how this new opportunity came about. For part 2 you'll tell a story about how someone just like them didn't believe it was possible, but then discovered it was. Then for part 3 you'll break down the number one objection people will have about this new opportunity you've presented them.

Step 3: Trial Close

This is something that you should be doing in between each story, but most certainly after you've gone through the three part story sequence.

What this does? Confirms that you still hold authority and that people are willing to take action when you ask them to.

Here are some easy, but solid examples:

"Are you guys getting this?"

This drives home the fact that yes they are getting what you're saying and they're agreeing that they are getting something. Like your offer you're about to pitch them.

Soft, subtle and important trial closes like this help tremendously when presenting your offer to your audience. It's a lot less awkward and they're somewhat prepared to be pitched.

Step 4: Close

Your close needs to match your personality or it'll simply be awkward. You can't be goofy, fun and loving and then all of a sudden out of nowhere tell them that their entire family is counting on them and if they don't take action they're a loser. It just doesn't fit the personality.

I'll let you in on a little secret as long as you promise to take action with it...

...the best closes happen when no one knows they're being closed.

This constitutes a few things:

1. Smooth
2. Effortless
3. Relevant

Here's what that means...

There are multiple parts to a script and when you can smoothly transition from stories to closing, you're golden. Want an example? Of course you do.

... if you can see exactly how I went from more than 6 figures in debt to becoming one of the world's highest paid copywriters go ahead and take action now by clicking the button below. By clicking that button you will open up the secret door that has been hiding all of the information, resources and support you'll need to travel the exact same path I have in just six weeks.

Smooth. No bumps, no stutters, no doubts... just pure smoothness. Think of the smoothest person you've ever met. Does your close sound like it would come out of there mouth?

If not, you need to rework it until it does.

Effortless...

If your close doesn't come across effortless as if you're not even trying to close someone... then your close is most likely too strong for the situation and you didn't do a good enough job leading up to the close.

Relevant...

Play off of the stories that have been told. The close is not a time to create a new story... it's to look back to previously told stories. This is your time to shine.

Step 5: Close Some More!

Now that you believe you've closed your audience it's time to go back and do all of that work I was telling you not to do before.

You only get one chance to really drive home and close a mass amount of sales. This is your opportunity to pick up an additional 1-10% of your conversions.

The best way to really work this in is to write down the top 5 objections your audience will have and work them into this part of the close. You can do this is an FAQ or Q&A or simply telling a story of a successful person using your product or service that had the same objection.

Here's the framework:

For those of you still here that haven't taken action quite yet here's a bonus I'm willing to throw in right now only...

Give them a bonus that overcomes an objection.

It's that easy!

Example:

Objection: Won't Make Money Back Fast Enough

Close: If you don't make your money back in 7 days or less I'll refund your entire purchase and let you keep the program!

Again... do not lie here. Be genuine they will see through your lies and honestly, liars never sustain anything they gain through deceptive practices anyways.

Putting each piece in the proper place will put you closer and closer to writing a wildly profitable webinar script. Don't be afraid of highlighting, taking notes and referencing this chapter everytime you write webinar scripts!

SECTION FIVE
OUTBOX $$$

CHAPTER 14
COLD EMAIL

If I could count the amount of times I'm asked by people about how to craft cold emails to generate thousands of piping hot leads I'd have... well I have made a lot of money doing just that.

Not only writing these cold emails myself, but teaching others how to do the same. You're probably wondering ... "How on earth can you predictably generate leads using cold email?" and that's precisely what you'll be uncovering in this chapter. So be sure to pay attention to every word as you read through these pages.

Now the biggest thing you have to remember about email marketing in general is two things:

- No one wants a promotional email in their inbox.
- No one wants a promotional email in their inbox.

Yeah, I repeated it over and over again because the number one mistake anyone and everyone makes when writing emails is simple. They try too hard to sound like a marketer.

Stop trying to sound like a marketer. No one likes marketers besides business owners who hired a good one ;).

So what do I mean when I say "no one wants a promotional email in their inbox?"

Don't be spammy. Your email needs to appear as if it is coming from a co-worker or potential customer... etc. Not from a vendor or someone trying to sell them shit.

So here is how to set yourself up for success to generate leads from cold email:

** DISCLAIMER **

I have no idea what the current cold email laws are at the time of you reading this book. At the time of writing this book it is okay to conduct cold emails to businesses as long as you follow the CAN-SPAM rules. I am in no way, shape or form giving you any legal advice and you should most certainly run these methods by your own attorney to make sure you're in compliance before you hit the "send button."

Alright, another legal disclaimer out of the way which means my lawyers are happy.

Now back to how I've helped generate thousands upon thousands of leads leveraging cold email.

I can't just tell you how to write the copy because honestly that'd be a disservice. I have to explain the entire process from start to finish so you can get a full understanding of how to make a successful cold email campaign.

Consider this... a bonus of sorts.

There are 3 parts to any email campaign that you must fight hard for.

Part 1: Getting into the inbox
Part 2: Getting opens
Part 3: Getting them to take action.

Part 1: Getting into the inbox

Before you go blasting off sending thousands of cold emails think about what your email service provider is going to think of that. Will they like you sending the same message to thousands of people at the same time?

Or will they think it's spam...

... yeah you guessed right.

So you have to in most scenarios "warm up the ip" which basically means you have to send small quantities of emails like 5, 10 or even 25 at a time over a 7 day period increasing amounts in small increments.

This will eventually allow you to send out 1,000 to 2,000 emails per day effectively and you'll have a stronger opportunity to get into more inboxes more often.

Now there are services out there that will allow you to blast millions at a time... think for a second if that will actually work for you or not.

I'm not saying it won't, I'm just saying you should really think about the big picture here before you go blasting off and burning ips, domains and email lists up.

More tricks to get into the inbox would be encouraging replies from the emails you first send in small increments. This jacks your delivery rate up quite a bit and makes you a trusted sender in most cases.

Part 2: Getting Opens

Make your "From" name your actual name. Sounds crazy right? You should experiment with your first name, first and last, last name, and other names. This increases the likelihood of them actually opening this email up in the first place.

The next part of getting people to open your email is your subject line. When you're emailing businesses you have to keep in mind that they are busy and emails are a time consuming part of the process. So, your subject line needs to sell them on why they should open you instead of delete you.

Here's my best subject line to date: Clients?

Yeah, one word with a question mark. Why? Because it intrigues business owners to want to open it up and figure out what you mean by

"Clients?" Or at least that's why I believe it works. Feel free to steal it for yourself!

Part 3: Getting them to take action

Keeping in mind that businesses are often busy or should be at least. You only have about 2 sentences to convince them to take action before they leave. I can promise they will not be reading your long winded email that is a huge sales pitch.

So wrap up what result you'll be providing and encourage an action. I recommend to encourage a reply here... but you can encourage whatever you'd like as your CTA.

Now that you know how to whip up some high converting cold emails and get them into inboxes and even opened... it's time for you to give it a shot.

CHAPTER 15
FOLLOW UP EMAIL SEQUENCES

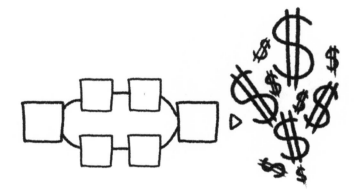

A lot of marketers either love email marketing or they hate email marketing. Regardless of your stance on email marketing the numbers simply don't lie.

According to a study complete right around the time I'm writing this book, on average if you spent $1.00 on email marketing you would squeeze out $44.00.[7]

Remember, the goal of marketing is simply to put $1.00 in and take $2.00 out. So if emails are producing $44.00 in revenue per $1.00 spent... well... I'd say the ROI is pretty decent and I'm sure you would to.

So let's dive into an actual framework you can apply to your follow up emails that if applied correctly could generate you a ton of cash and make you filthy rich and at the very least will improve some conversions and add additional sales into your business.

There are really 3 steps to writing a powerful email sequence that can produce insane results.

Step 1: Know Why They Didn't Buy

I can't tell you how many times I've critiqued copy or had someone come to me and ask why they weren't picking up a single sale from their follow up emails like their guru said they would.
I ask them all the same question:

"Why didn't they buy in the first place?"

They all answered pretty similarly. "I'm not sure."

or

"I think ... "

Both are very very very wrong answers. In order for you to really drive home and add additional sales through follow up emails you have to understand why they didn't buy the first time.

Here's why...

If you have a clear understanding of someone who went through your process and then didn't purchase anything... you'll know how to overcome it in the next two steps.

Which brings us into the next step.

Step # 2: List Top Reasons They Didn't Buy

Here's what this means:

You should have a list of maybe 10 reasons why they didn't purchase. You then need to choose three of the most powerful reasons and put a star next to them. These reasons are actually objections and you're going to overcome them as if you've been a sales professional your entire life and know exactly what to say.

It's kind of like when you're shopping for cars. You go into the dealership, you talk to a sales person. They show you some cars you have to think about it and you leave without buying. They then call you up offering some insane discount their manager just came up with that's good for today only.

Most of the time this will work if you're actually interested in the car. The sales person in this scenario picked the most common objection and overcame it in his follow up. Just like you should with your email follow ups.

Step # 3: Ask For A Reply

In the example above the car salesman tried overcoming the most common objection people have when buying cars. Here's what that looks like when they're told no...

They start asking questions like "What's the 1 thing keeping you from buying this car right now?"

How can you do that? Well, you ask them to reply or to schedule a call with you. This is supposed to be very, very, very low pressure and simply to gain more insight on what the true objection is. Remember we talked about the 8 reasons people buy. Find one of them that is important to your potential customer and close them on it.

Remember, statistics show 80% of sales (across every industry) are made on the 12th contact. Don't waste money and time by retargeting them over and over again to hit that 12th contact... use automated email sequences that push them to buy. (I'm not saying to never run retargeting campaigns... I'm simply suggesting to use automated emails to pick up sales you would have missed out on.)

HIDDEN CHAPTER

Because you're here and still reading this book I figured I'd give you an exclusive invite. Remember back to the beginning of this book where I talked about the statistics of those that don't make it all the way through a book?

Well you're not just another statistic. In fact, you're the opposite. You're apart of the small 1% of the world that values growth.

I put this hidden chapter in here for a few reasons:

1. Because you're a badass.
2. Because I'm a badass.

Here's what I mean:

Writing copy can honestly be learned by reading a book. It is entirely possible. However, if you don't read the entire thing and take notes and follow instructions... it's nearly impossible.

I wanted to break down some A-List secrets of writing copy that I didn't mention in this book at all until now.

Fair enough?

In fact,

I even put together everything I'm about to talk about in a video format.

You can access the free no cost training at:

writelikethewolf.com/hiddenchapter

There are a few bonuses inside of that no cost training that you may want to get your hands on if you really want to take your copywriting skills to the next level.

Let's dive in shall we?

Obtaining "A-List" status as a copywriter is challenging for a large number of reasons.

The main reason being that there isn't a single university or "coach" bringing any copywriters up to A-List status consistently.

So there is no proper structure or process to follow to reach it. However, I believe there is a way to consistently help others reach this level and I've been doing so inside of my secret Writing Academy.

No, I'm not selling you into my academy or telling you it's the only way to become an A-Lister. I'm simply saying that I believe I've cracked that code and if you place your trust in me and follow the directions in this book with a bit of out of the box style of thinking you'll be knocking down million dollar campaigns on auto-pilot.

In order to really get to that coveted "A-List" status we must dive deep. I mean... real deep.

If we look at copywriting from a thirty thousand foot view there's a few basics that we must master.

The first is to obsess over psychology, but more so the way humans make decisions. Not just because of the emotional stuff that we talked about in previous chapters, but how those emotions come about and how you can trigger them on command.

There are many many many free resources out there covering psychology at the highest levels. As crazy as it sounds there are even a few lectures from Harvard University on the topic. A little bit of digging here and a lot of information will turn up.

The next thing you'll need to obsess over is NLP or Neuro Linguistic Programming. Neuro refers to your neurology; Linguistic refers to language; programming refers to how that language functions. In other words, learning NLP is kind of like learning the language of the mind.

When you begin to understand how the mind operates you can better use your newfound psychology knowledge of how to trigger those emotions on command effortlessly.

Another really big factor I've studied quite a bit that has helped me a lot in writing really high converting ad copy is how Hostage Negotiators win every time without giving anything in return.

Understanding how they are able to negotiate and win everything and give up nothing gives you a unique perspective to sales and negotiating in general that you can incorporate into your ad copy in the right scenarios.

A really good reference for this is Mr. Chris Voss himself. Former FBI Hostage Negotiator of a few decades who has a best selling book titled: "Never Split The Difference."

Mr. Voss has plenty of free content floating around the internet including a blog, weekly email and even a YouTube channel. You'll want to be sure you're following him closely so you too can get people to do everything you want without giving them anything they way in exchange. (your friends will love it... not.)

One of the next things that you should consider looking into and studying would be deception. Deception is to cause (someone) to believe something that is not true, typically in order to gain some personal advantage. In other words, deception is lying.

Understanding when people lie and why they're lying can help you tremendously with persuasion for a few reasons. First reason is quite simple, the majority of the world lies because they feel they must lie in order to fit in. In other words people lie because they don't want to feel embarrassed. The next reason is because it will help you better understand human emotion and what happens when people feel a certain way. Those feelings and how they happen can help tremendously bridge the gap between the new psychology, nlp and hostage negotiation tactics you've began to study.

Now I feel this goes without saying, but I have not a shred of proof that anything I talked about in this chapter is guaranteed to help you achieve "A-List" status. All I can do is share with you what I've personally studied and obsessed over that I often reference to write winning ad copy for myself and my clients over and over and over again helping produce tens of millions of dollars in revenue.

I hope this chapter was of great help to you and if it did indeed peak your interest and you wanted a bit deeper of an explanation of what was discussed in this chapter please, go to:

writelikethewolf.com/hiddenchapter

so you can consume the no cost mini training I did on each of these topics.

It will never cost you a dime.

And that's all I have for you guys for now!

Thank you so much for taking the time to read every last word in this book. I hope this book has transformed your life as much as writing it has transformed mine.

Feel free to leave a review on Amazon or tag me on social media: @colevandee

Links to articles for research:

1. charfen.com
2. nyti.ms/2SuWv8M
3. bit.ly/2N3qizH
4. bit.ly/2DAtw9s
5. frankkernbook.com
6. bit.ly/2TNLwUN
7. bit.ly/2XabyDM
8. bit.ly/2SKES4p

About The Author

Instead of writing this in the third person like most authors do I'd much rather tell you from my perspective. Fair enough?

As you've probably figured out by now, my name is Cole VanDeWoestyne and most people refer to me as *The Wolf of Copywriting*. It could be because I've made them millions of dollars or because they've seen a lot of my content I've put out there or I've helped them hone their skills of copywriting in a matter of minutes or months (depending on if they hired me to coach them or just messaged me on Facebook for help.) Regardless of what aspect I've helped someone that's what I'm most proud of. Yes, helping people. Legitimately.

I didn't write this book to become a millionaire. In fact, I didn't write this book necessarily to make a single dollar from it. I wrote this book and spent money to get it into your hands because as I age I learn more and more that life is more rewarding when you help others win. And I know that when people just like you pick this book up, read it cover to cover and absorb every ounce of knowledge they can out of it and then they apply it... they win.

So thank you for making the decision to change your life for the better. It really means a lot to me that you made that decision.

And if you're still reading this I'd like to make a suggestion that may take everything you just learned another step further...

... I do have a full on Copywriting Boot Camp.

It's a 6-Week program that is pre-recorded so you can work at your own pace. It goes so deep in fact that I actually uploaded over 50+ videos that average nearly 10-15 minutes each. That's over 12 hours of content PLUS a ton of bonuses.

I don't know if you're the kind of person that would be interested in something like that or not...

... but if you are you can head over to writelikethewolf.com/invest to sign up.

As a token of my appreciation...

use the code BOOK for a $500 coupon.

Made in the USA
Columbia, SC
25 July 2024

39305504R00138